MERCY REIGN

- THE UNCONDITIONAL LOVE,
- COMPASSIONATE
- AND IMMENSE KINDNESS OF GOD TO EVERYONE

BLESSING E. BASSEY

Gotham Books
30 N Gould St.
Ste. 20820, Sheridan, WY 82801
https://gothambooksinc.com/
Phone: 1 (307) 464-7800

Published by Gotham Books (date published Feb 2022)

ISBN: 978-1-956349-20-7 (sc)
ISBN: 978-1-956349-21-4 (e)

Library of Congress Control Number: 2022901923

CONTENTS

CHAPTER ONE

MERCY REIGN: OVER FAMILY FOUNDATION

God's mercy surpasses all sins you have ever committed, is committing and will ever commit. Though, for the fact that His mercies have already covered our sins is not a license for us to continue in sin; Paul asked a question in the book of Romans 6:1, he says "shall we continue in sin that grace may abound? Do you think it is proper to sin when you are conscious of it before ever committing that sin? Like it is popularly held among some believers today that the blood of Jesus has already paid the price for all our sins and therefore no one can condemn anyone when they sin. Wait a moment, have you ever thought about if that person should die while still on the act of committing that sin? The mercies of God though reign above the condemnation of the devil, we still have to fear God and depart from evil and iniquity. This chapter will be discussing on how the blood of Jesus has reign over our family foundation of idol worshipping, secret cult, incest, curses, evil, satanic and demonic covenant entered into by our forefathers, grandfathers and immediate parents. Most of our forefathers made a serious covenant with the devil for various reasons such as money, power, positions of authorities ranging from political to personal, fame and so many other things, they vow to serve the devil and made a deal with him which is now affecting their decedents, which 2…232xyou and I belongs.

A lot of us Christians are facing one or two spiritual battles we do not know where it's coming or even what we are fighting. It is written in Psalm 11:3-7, that if the foundation be destroy what can the righteous do? Most often when preachers make this comments from the scripture, making it look like we that affected by such evil or curse foundation are doom for life, I often respond "the righteous can pray". Do you know why I always say this? Because prayer is the only way to change circumstances. With prayer, heaven can intervene in your case and repair the damaged foundation. In short, because of the mercies of God, the blood of Jesus can and its capable of not only changing your foundation but is also able to give you a new foundation. Mercy reign over all kinds of foundation being cursed, polluted by incest or ancestral covenant with the devil or evil spirits. I have seen families whose forefathers had a deal with the devil for generations but as soon as a new generation came forth and assess their lives and perceive that something was wrong about their lives, they cry to God for a change or a new foundation, and eventually changing their foundation from the devils hold or idolatry to God's foundation. What am saying is that, the children of the new generation made a decision contrarily to that of their forefathers, grandparent or parent and entered a new covenant with the blood of Jesus. The convent of Christ is the covenant of peace joy, abundance, divine health, healing, holiness, sanctification, and **Isaiah 53:5 – But he was wounded for our transgressions, he was bruised for our iniquities: the chastisement of our peace was upon him; and with his stripes we are healed.6 All we like sheep have gone astray; we have turned every one to his own way; and the Lord hath laid on him the iniquity of us all.**

7 He was oppressed, and he was afflicted, yet he opened not his mouth: he is brought as a lamb to the slaughter, and as a sheep before her shearers is dumb, so he openeth not his mouth.

2 Corinthians 5:18 - And all things are of God, who hath reconciled us to himself by Jesus Christ, and hath given to us the ministry of reconciliation;

His mercy surpasses our sin? iniquities or sins of your father's house, that is, the sin of your foundation have been taken care of by the shedding and sacrifice of the blood of Jesus on the cross of Calvary. Jesus on the cross became sin for us (both past, present and future sins) so that we can be free from every form of sin, as a result of this great sacrifice, there became no need for any other sacrifice of goat, bulls or human. The blood of Jesus Christ shed on the cross became the seal to all other sacrifice. Despite the sins of your foundation which hitherto made you an enemy of God has been taken care of on the cross of Calvary, 2 Corinthian 5:18 above states that the blood shed for us on the cross has reconcile us back to God as new creatures, pure and without blemishes, wrinkles or spots. Jesus has presented us to God as a beauty to behold. When mercy reign, God sees us as treasures to cherish and we need to see ourselves the way He sees us. Whenever am alone, all I do is to imagine how God loves me and what he has invested in me even before I was born or conceived. I might have gone through trials but also know that there are people that have gone through worst trials in life and by the mercies of God they still smile and still love others just as Christ loved them. Whenever I think about Pastor Joyce Meyer past and present, I just wonder aloud " what a merciful God we serve". Our foundation cannot completely alter our God ordain future unless we fail to do what God wants us to do or embrace his mercies. Pastor Joyce Meyer to me is operating in the mercies of God. The mercy of God has reign over her past live of incest her father committed with her. A lot of people today believe that the problems they are facing in life is as a result of the sin of incest intheir family, but the question is, what are they doing about it? like Joyce Meyer, did they take it to God and ask for mercy by pleading the blood of Jesus against that sin? Like she said, the sin of incest has been in her foundation, her father was also abused as a child by a family member, so, it just continues but a generation like Joyce Meyer has to break that curse. God helped her and she broke it over her children's live and generation. Whatever foundation you came from, please plead the blood of mercy, for the blood speaks restoration and a new beginning for us all.

Hebrews 12:24 - And to Jesus the mediator of the new covenant, and to the blood of sprinkling, that speaketh better things than that of Abel.

Generational curses can be broken beginning with you, you need to make a choice. The bible says generation curse can last up to the fourth generation but the mercies can also last forever or many more years.

Psalm 103:17 – 18 - But the mercy of the Lord is from everlasting to everlasting upon them that fear him, and his righteousness unto children's children; 18 To such as keep his covenant, and to those that remember his commandments to do them.

Let see another story of one person in the bible breaking generational curse or cursed foundation.

In 2 chronicles 22:11-12 and 2 kings 1, there is a woman name Jehosheba meaning" Jehovah is my oath". Jehosheba was the daughter of King Jehoram, or Joram, by his secondary wife, half-sister of King Ahaziah. She became the wife of the high priest, Jehoiada, and is the only instance of a princess marrying a high priest. Queens Athaliah who happen to be a very wicked witch and also from a generation of witches, decides one day to kill all her children including grandchildren because she was afraid that they might take after her evil ways. But Jehiosheba went and took one of the grandchildren which was also her nephew (king Ahaziah is the husband of Athaliah) hid him for six years while others were killed. She and her husband raised her nephew (name Jehoash) in the first temple built by Solomon. Jehoash grew up and changed the history of his family; he became a child of God and follows the ways of God. He was crowned a new king of Judah inside the temple of God and the good news is that Christ lineage came from this generation. The curse was changed to blessing.

Can you imagine, where one woman thought it was over with her and her generation including decedents because of foundational sins or curses of witchcraft, another woman saw an opportunity to change the foundation from evil to good?

Even those surrounded by evil people can serve God! Jehosheba grew up in an environment that was saturated with evil. The one God of the Scriptures was rejected. In her life "environment" did not dictate her choices. She stood apart from family, from friends and chose to serve God. She knew that her choices were in direct conflict with what her family wanted, but she chose to follow God and separate from family. This is a difficult decision and many are unwilling to make it. Jehosheba reminds us today that if we are to follow God then we must choose to follow Him even if it means conflict with family (culled from Personalities Of The Old Testament, www.churchesofchrist.net).

There might be a curse of insanity, anger or suicide in your family but remembers what Jesus said on the cross "it is finished"   . If a woman can so have faith in God in the old testament and was able to change a whole generational curse, then what are we waiting for when we have the blood of Jesus that has reconcile us back to God.   This   season pray like you have never before or if you are sure you have been delivered from cursed foundation, then start giving God glory and praise him.

We all remember Ruth in the bible (the book of Ruth), she lived to change her life by following and accepting the lord as her God. She had a cursed foundation and was from a people that was cursed by God himself but how amazing she made it. She lived to change the lives of her descendants. God had no choice than to have mercy on her because of her love for God and the people of God. You too like Ruth, Joyce Meyer and others can turn from the evil ways of your family or generation to God.

CHAPTER TWO

MERCY REIGN: OVER PAST SINS, MISTAKES AND FUTURE SINS

God will not get rid of you because of your sins. Like Joyce Meyer once liken our sinful lives sometimes to a dog (pet) that poos and will keep cleaning up the poo without getting offended and return them to their pet pound, the same way God will not send us away because we sinned, he will keep cleaning our poo till we grow up and learn to stop pooing on the floor. He encourages us to come closer just as we do to our dog and kids when they fall. When our kids starts walking they fall several times and most times they have to be supported by their parent or a guardian to prevent them from falling, the same way God sometimes guards us preventing us from falling but even when we fall, just like our parents or guardian, he still picks us up. This is exactly what mercy does for us, mercy picks us up and dust us and cleanse us. Like the dog that poos, no matter the smell, God still loves us and more than willing to keep us. Past sin should not drive us away from God.

God needs you knowing you are a donkey that fall into the ditch sometimes but the good news is that you are God's donkey. Psalm 23 says the lord is our Shepherd, we are the sheep in His sheepfold and this is the reason we need to show mercy to others because Jesus showed mercy to us. We all make mistakes and we don't have to be down because of that, when we are down it affect our relationship with others and our God. We need to devout ourselves and move on knowing that God's mercies prevail over our mistakes and any judgment anyone might want to pass on us. It is okay for us to feel remorse about our sin and repent before God, we do not need to feel guilty and remain guilty. When we feel guilty for a long to time without repenting, we should know it's the devil that is operating and not God. The devil makes us feel guilty in order for him to keep us in a state that God does not want us to be, when we are emotionally down we will not be able to experience or feel the presence of God. We will be unable to move forward in life because the devil will always remind us of sin we committed that even God has long forgiven us.

Hebrews 8:12 - For I will be merciful to their unrighteousness, and their sins and their iniquities will I remember no more.

If God says he will be merciful to our sins, unrighteousness and iniquities and that he will never again remember them, do we for any reason thinks he is lying or can't forgive us or that He is not capable to forgive and not remember? Man can forgive and still remember but be rest assure that whatever God says He will do He will do it. If He says He has forgiven us, then that is it, we need to believe Him and have faith to move on.

8 The Lord is merciful and gracious, slow to anger, and plenteous in mercy.

9 He will not always chide: neither will he keep his anger forever.

10 He hath not dealt with us after our sins; nor rewarded us according to our iniquities.

11 For as the heaven is high above the earth, so great is his mercy toward them that fear him.

12 As far as the east is from the west, so far hath he removed our transgressions from us.

13 Like as a father pitieth his children, so the Lord pitieth them that fear him.

14 For he knoweth our frame; he remembereth that we are dust.

From the above scripture, we will find that God's anger is only temporal (verse 9), though he is very slow in getting angry with our wrong doings, yet even when he gets angry, it is only for a moment but his mercy is everlasting. We can see in verse 10 that our God does not deal with us according to our sins nor has he rewarded us according our iniquities. God does not count our disobedience, mistakes or sins, rather the bible says that as the heavens are higher than the earth so great is his mercy towards those that fear him. The psalmist went on to say that as a father pity his son so that lord pity those that fear him. A natural father is always out to protect his son against anything thing that will cause or bring shame to him (the father) through his son. Most father go as far as looking out for the kind of friends or company their children keeps and also take interest in the affairs of their son.

Whatever your past lifestyle, God has forgiven you and He is able to clean you and start afresh with you, for He is a merciful God. You need to acknowledge this and put behind all past sins, unrighteousness and iniquities without referring to them or even when you do refer to them, it will be to glorify the name of God by sharing it as a testimony to help somebody and edify the body of Christ. Prostitutes, drug addicts, harmed rubbers and a host of deviants who after leaving their past lifestyle came to God with total surrender and have converted many people to Christ just with their testimonies. There is no soldier or army of Christ that hasn't got a scar because do you what? God will not commit greatness to an untested solider. If you are a true soldier of Christ, then you must have gone through life knowing fully well that God got your back, His mercies saw you through life and it's still seeing you through.

In the book of Mathew 12:3-8 tells how David and his men were very hungry and entered the house of God and ate the showbread meant for the priest which was not lawful for David nor his men to eat, yet the bible said nothing negative or evil happened to them, because Jesus telling his disciples this story was being accused by the Pharisees that His (Jesus) disciples were plucking and eating corn on the Sabbath day which was unlawful to them. But Jesus Christ made the Pharisees to understand the He (Jesus) is the lord of the Sabbath and that greater than the Sabbath is here. And Jesus told the Pharisees that if they had known the meaning of the phrase "I will have mercy not sacrifice", they would not have condemned the guiltless. We need to know according to this scripture, that as Jesus is lord over the Sabbath day so also is God's mercy lord over our past sins, present sin and mistakes.

MATHEW 12:1-8 At that time Jesus went on the sabbath day through the corn; and his disciples were an hungred, and began to pluck the ears of corn and to eat.

2 But when the Pharisees saw it, they said unto him, Behold, thy disciples do that which is not lawful to do upon the sabbath day.

3 But he said unto them, Have ye not read what David did, when he was an hungred, and they that were with him;

4 How he entered into the house of God, and did eat the shewbread, which was not lawful for him to eat, neither for them which were with him, but only for the priests?

5 Or have ye not read in the law, how that on the sabbath days the priests in the temple profane the sabbath, and are blameless?

6 But I say unto you, That in this place is one greater than the temple.

7 But if ye had known what this meaneth, I will have mercy, and not sacrifice, ye would not have condemned the guiltless.

8 For the Son of man is Lord even of the sabbath day.

In life there are many Pharisees that will want to accuse us of doing things unlawful or trying to make us feel guilty of our action just like what they were about to do to the disciples before Jesus intervened and stopped the Pharisees. What this bible passage is telling us is that God will only weight our reason and motive behind our action and not just our action. Remember the disciples were very hungry before they started plucking the corn to eat; and this also applies to David and his men, they were equally hungry before they eat the bread meant for the priest. Jesus also gave example of the priest that profane the Sabbath day and were declared blameless because of mercy. Pity yourself over a mistake made in the past? Maybe about your marriage, relationship, career, kids, ministry or what do you think God is not able to redeem by the power of his mercy? Just as the disciples, David and his men continue their lives like nothing had happened, the same way God is asking you to continue your life because HIS MERCY REIGN.

This reminds me of my four year old daughter, whenever she does anything bad and am about to get angry with her, she always say, mummy please, I didn't mean it or I didn't mean to do that, and I always believe her and stop my action immediately. And the look on her eyes alone puts off my anger immediately. Know what? I want to believe that God always look down from heaven and see how afraid and shaken we are when we are doing things we might consider are unlawful to him. Many times I have done things contrarily to what God wants, however, like the disciples, they were never intentional and I look up to heaven and ask Him for mercy and strength to carry on.

In the book of Leviticus we were told that when the children of Israel sin against God, a bull is usually offered as a sacrifice to atone for their sins. What is usually done is that the sins of the people is spiritually transfer to the bull by the priest laying his hands on the head of the bull confessing the sins of the people on the bull, after which the bull is killed and its blood used to appease God to turn away his anger, and this ritual is done yearly.

Leviticus 4:13-21 King James Version (KJV)

13 And if the whole congregation of Israel sin through ignorance, and the thing be hid from the eyes of the assembly, and they have done somewhat against any of the commandments of the Lord concerning things which should not be done, and are guilty;

14 When the sin, which they have sinned against it, is known, then the congregation shall offer a young bullock for the sin, and bring him before the tabernacle of the congregation.

15 And the elders of the congregation shall lay their hands upon the head of the bullock before the Lord: and the bullock shall be killed before the Lord.

16 And the priest that is anointed shall bring of the bullock's blood to the tabernacle of the congregation:

17 And the priest shall dip his finger in some of the blood, and sprinkle it seven times before the Lord, even before the vail.

18 And he shall put some of the blood upon the horns of the altar which is before the Lord, that is in the tabernacle of the congregation, and shall pour out all the blood at the bottom of the altar of the burnt offering, which is at the door of the tabernacle of the congregation.

19 And he shall take all his fat from him, and burn it upon the altar.

20 And he shall do with the bullock as he did with the bullock for a sin offering, so shall he do with this: and the priest shall make an atonement for them, and it shall be forgiven them.

21 And he shall carry forth the bullock without the camp, and burn him as he burned the first bullock: it is a sin offering for the congregation.

Oh! I have a good news for you, do you know that instead of the animal bull, Jesus came and took the place of the bull to die once and for all for the remission and atonement of our sins both past, present and in the future? My friend, what kind of sin have you committed or you are still committing that you think its too big for God to forgive, listen you are already been forgiven. All you need to do is stay away from sin. According to the book of Mathew20;28, Christ came to give his live as a ransom for many, and that many includes you and I.

Matthew 20:28 - Even as the Son of man came not to be ministered unto, but to minister, and to give his life a ransom for many.

Remember in the book of Genesis when Adam and eve sinned against God, God prepare an animal skin and used it as a covering to cover their nakedness. He covered them knowing what they were about to face outside the garden of Eden.

God wants us to learn how, in mercy, He had prepared the world to receive the One whose blood would provide that adequate covering for us. He would deliver us and protect us from the wrath that is to come. He would die and pay the price, the ransom for Adam and his descendants' sin once and for all. He wants us to learn that, by killing the animals whose skins He used to provide clothing for Adam and Eve, He had demonstrated the method by which He would provide redemption and salvation for Adam and his descendants. This is why

Jesus Christ is refer to as our substitute, because he became a substitute for us, he took our place of sin and gave us His righteousness. The blood of Jesus shed of us has become our covering, and His covering is everlasting, it is permanent and never to be altered, changed or removed.

As you are reading this book, I want you to know that the blood of Jesus reigns over you as a covering on every area of your life and family. It was one thing to judge the sinners, but it was something completely different to cover, to remove their sins from His sight (cf. Habbakkuk 1: 13). But your sin has already been removed from the sight of God and you longer need any priest to stand in gap as an intermediary between you and God, for the blood of Jesus has not become your intermediary. The bible says Jesus Christ is seated at the right hand of God in the heavenly places acting as an advocate for you and I. All you need to do whenever you sin or come short of God's glory is to pray through Jesus for the mercy, no matter the degree or lever of sin. Atonement, the covering, the removal of sin, is spoken of in the Old Testament of the Bible approximately one hundred times. The first time it occurs is in Genesis 6: 14, where God instructed Noah, with reference the preparation of the ark, to "cover it inside and outside with pitch." The blood of the sacrifice was to be used to "cover over" so that the sin was hidden from God's sight, with the implication that the sin is wiped away in the process. But the blood of Jesus has covered us all round both inside and outside.

A lot of people believe they are being punish for their past sins and mistakes, this a lie from the pit of hell, and the devil who is the father of all liar is responsible for this lie for it is written in the book of Romans 8:1, that there is therefore now no condemnation to them that are in Christ Jesus for it is God that judge. Never again should you allow anyone condemn you because each day you live, you live to the glory of God and whatsoever you do, you do it to the glory of God.

CHAPTER THREE

MERCY REIGN: OVER WEAKNESSES

In talking about weakness, what do we consider as weakness maybe what others see as smartness or wisdom? I know as you read this chapter you will be expecting me to write about weaknesses such as alcoholic, drug addiction, stealing, prostituting and others. But I will like to go through the under-listed questions and answer for ourselves which question applies to us and at the end of this chapter pray about them by pleading the blood of mercy.

QUESTIONS:

- ✓ Have you ever said the wrong thing and wished with all your heart that you could retract the statement?
- ✓ Have you ever gossiped, revealed a confidence, or passed on a rumor that caused a problem for others?
- ✓ Have you ever misjudged a person or situation and later came to see that your judgment was wrong, and because of your wrong judgment, the individual felt separated from others and hurt?
- ✓ Have you ever judged another correctly as being wrong, but failed to consider the individual's background and what they have had to overcome?

- ✓ Have you ever taken God's job and passed a condemning judgment on another person?
- ✓ Have you ever had a poor attitude that caused you to be unforgiving toward a fellow member of the church?
- ✓ Have you ever looked down on someone who seemed never to be able to get things right and who continually slipped in the same areas over and over, and because of this, you felt free to be critical of them? *All questions was culled from Mercy: The Better Option by John O. Reid Forerunner, "Ready Answer," January-February 2010*

We are likely all guilty of these sins many times over and over again. Sometimes because we feel we have arrive at a particular destination, we tend to look down on others that are still on their way or journey to where we currently are. No matter what questions apply to us, we should know that the blood of Jesus is able to help us overcome these weaknesses. I decide to choose this set of weaknesses for the simple fact that they are not obvious weaknesses. Remember Peter in the bible telling Jesus that he will never betrayed Jesus and that even if anyone should abandon Jesus he will never abandon him. What Peter was doing here was simply judging the person who was going to betrayed Jesus without knowing that he too is capable of doing same but Jesus was protecting him, remember Jesus told him that the devil is very determine to sieve Peter but He (Jesus) has prayed for him that his faith fails not? At the end what did we see Peter did? Of cause, he denied Jesus three times. But the good news again is that Jesus has already forgiven them all of any future sins because he knows their weaknesses more than they do. How did he forgive them of all future sins including the one who betrayed him, he washed their foots, a sign of his mercy and forgiveness. When Peter asked Jesus if he will wash is his also, Jesus replied and said if I do not wash your feet you have no part with me. ***John 13:1-2 Now before the feast of the passover, when Jesus knew that his hour was come that he should depart out of this world unto the Father, having loved his own which were in the world, he loved them unto the end. And*** *supper being ended, the devil having now put into the heart of Judas Iscariot, Simon's son, to betray him;*

John 13:3-8 - He riseth from supper, and laid aside his garments; and took a towel, and girded himself. After that he poureth water into a bason, and began to wash the disciples' feet, and to wipe them with the towel wherewith he was girded. Then cometh he to Simon Peter: and Peter saith unto him, Lord, dost thou wash my feet? Jesus answered and said unto him, What I do thou knowest not now; but thou shalt know hereafter. Peter saith unto him, Thou shalt never wash my feet. Jesus answered him, If I wash thee not, thou hast no part with me.

Jesus is still in the business of washing our feet today and he is still going to wash our feet in the future. Whatever our weaknesses maybe all we need do is to change and think about how Jesus loves us and cover us with his blood of mercy so we too should do the same to others by showing mercy when they fail or not performing up to our standard.

The book of James 2:12-13 urges us to show mercy to others because judgment is without mercy to those who have shown no mercy to others since Christ show mercy to us without passing judgment we ought also to do same to our fellow brothers and sisters and the entire human race on earth. If the book of Romans 8:1 says there is no condemnation to those who are in Christ Jesus, that means we cannot condemn others too. The verse 13 of James chapter 2 says mercy triumph over judgment, yes, this is true because the blood of Jesus plead mercy over every judgment the devil and his cohort will want to or has already passed upon us. Whatever anyone will do to us, it is important that we put on the bowel of mercy in readiness to forgive that person whether in the church or in the circular world, for God will only have mercy on whoever has shown mercy.

James 2:12-13 - 12 So speak and so do as those who will be judged by the law of liberty. 13 For judgment is without mercy to the one who has shown no mercy. Mercy triumphs over judgment.

In analyzing the above questions, we find that we have sometimes be judgmental about others actions, behavior and character without really knowing them. But despite our reason for taking part in any of the above question, Christ has already forgiven us and by virtue of the blood of Jesus we have be set free from every judgment. Irrespective of whatever our weaknesses may be whether alcoholic or drug addiction, the blood of mercy is able to set us free for such weaknesses are demonic attack and must therefore be fought against with the faith in God's power. 2 Corinthians 13:4 said Christ was crucified in weakness but yet he lives by God's power. The same thing applies to us, we need to live by God's divine power. In my life I have made almost all of the mistakes a person can make especially with my mouth, and since I realized this, I have truly appreciated those who have extended mercy to me by forgiving me. I have learnt a great lesson by their maturity in the way they handled it; I have therefore made up my mind to extend mercy and kindness to others.

2 Corinthians 13:4 - For to be sure, he was crucified in weakness, yet he lives by God's power. Likewise, we are weak in him, yet by God's power we will live with him in our dealing with you.

Let Christ be the judge, and do you know what? Christ will not judge you because he knows your frame that you are flesh and susceptible to sin, yes, the bible says he took the frame of man that he might experience what we feel, that is our weakness.

Philippians 2:7 - Rather, he made himself nothing by taking the very nature of a servant, being made in human likeness.

Sometimes in each of our lives we feel emotionally or physically weary, weak, or broken. We need to look upward to our Lord Jesus Christ and tell him how we feel and that we have nothing more to give or hold on to. Our sovereign God who is rich in mercy, has already provides us a remedy when we are facing these life experiences, because he said in 2 Corinthians 12:9, "My grace is sufficient for you, for my power is made perfect in weakness." We sometimes result to other things as a way out of our weaknesses but the truth is that we should turn to our only source of strength and let him give us the grace to carry on because of his mercy. When we find ourselves complaining, all we need do is turn to Him and ask for his mercy to help us at times like this.

Some years ago I used to complain about almost everything till the lord opened my eyes to see that complaining was a serious weakness that I have to deal with and overcome, by the mercy of God I was able to overcome it. the same thing gossiping, in this case, the lord spoke to me and said, it will not be good if I engage in gossiping because it will tarnish my image as a preacher and affect those who attends the fellowship I was heading. I had to pray and ask God for mercy, do you know that he truly helped me to the extent that my colleagues in the office noticed that whenever a topic about a co-worker is about to begin, I will just walk away without contributing even a word. Gossiping is a serious weakness but most of us Christian don't realize it, we just overlook it or take it for granted. We need God's mercy to reign over our weakness so that we can stand before God with a free heart without any burden.

It is through our weakness that the power of God's strength can flow most freely. Everything that surrounds us in our secular world abhors weakness; but the crystal truth is that some type or degree of weakness exists in each of us, some to me are inborn, just like anger and it can run from generation to generation. No matter how spiritual, rich, famous, powerful, educated or significant we may appear, some sort of weakness still prevail in our lives. Like in the case of Moses, the weakness of anger in his linage stopped him from entering the promise land. As we need to turn to god for mercy because as we have been saying his mercy reign over our weakness be it generational like in the case of Moses.

Weakness has no boundaries. At every level of society, in every race, ethnicity, and gender, we each possess weakness of some degree. Insecurities sometimes makes our weakness to surface like the weakness of pride and angers. Those that have the weakness of pride are actually very humble but they do it because they feel insecure. All the time, God gently calls us to let Him make our weakness into something good to glorify His name. We must be willing to allow God to use the circumstances of our lives to reach out to others. We must be a bridge for others to walk across, from their own darkness and pain into His healing Light, JUST BECAUSE MERCY REIGNS OVER WEAKNESS.

Like Paul, we do not have to run from our weakness or try to hid our weakness like they don't exit. Paul said in 2 Corinthians 12:9-10, **"9 And he said unto me, My grace is sufficient for thee: for my strength is made perfect in weakness. Most gladly therefore will I rather glory in my infirmities, that the power of Christ may rest upon me.**

10 Therefore I take pleasure in infirmities, in reproaches, in necessities, in persecutions, in distresses for Christ's sake: for when I am weak, then am I strong.

MAJOR AREAS OF WEAKNESS WHERE WE NEED GOD'S MERCY TO PREVAIL

- PRIDE
- BOASTFULNESS
- BACKBITING
- ANGER
- GOSSIP
- CONDERMING OTHERS
- SELF RIGHTUOUSNESS

The above list is endless and we alone know our weakness.

CHAPTER FOUR

MERCY REIGN: OVER POVERTY, LACK AND INSUFFICENCY

The mercy of God reign over poverty, lack and financial insufficiency, if Jesus said he has spiritually transfer his wealth and riches to us then in the physical, we should manifest his richness and live in abundance. Jesus came from a world and country flowing with milk and honey but because of you and I he chose to live a life of poverty by transferring to us his spiritual authority of wealth and riches. This great transfer was made at the cross of Calvary when all sins of man were heap on him. God did not initially create me to be poor but devil brought poverty to man as a result of man's sin at the Garden of Eden. The blood gushing out from the hand of Jesus signifies the transfer of his wealth to us. The blood is the blood of exchange; he shed the blood from his hand to cleanse our hands from every curse of poverty, lack and insufficiency. He exchanges his wealth for our poverty.

2 Corinthians 8:9 - For you know the grace of our Lord Jesus Christ, that though he was rich, yet for your sake he became poor, so that you through his poverty might become rich.

The cross is the place of the great exchange. The grace of God was release abundantly upon the cross of cavalry to us all to live above every form of degradation including poverty. The mercy of the blood of Jesus spoke against every form of sin induce poverty and as a matter of fact its still speaking today and will continue to speak till we see him and reign with him eternally.

Are you still thinking of how you are going to make financially in life? Or how you are going to break the yoke or curse of poverty upon your family? Has there been a generation curse of poverty in your family, that is, your forefathers, grandparents and even your father lived and die in poverty? All hope is not lost as Jesus has already done a thorough work in setting you free from every curse or yoke.

Galatian 3:13 - Christ hath redeemed us from the curse of the law, being made a curse for us: for it is written, Cursed is every one that hangeth on a tree:

Remember, the scripture above says that though Jesus Christ our lord and savior, though he was rich but for our sake became poor that through his poverty you and I might became rich. This scripture used the verb "might", that means if you are willing to break the curse of that poverty that is causing you pain in your life and family then will be set free. Though the mercy of the blood reigns over poverty, we as Christians still have to take position with God and take by force what belongs to us, we need to equipped and armed ourselves with scriptures telling us about our financial freedom base on the blood of mercy. The devil will fight back to prevent us from having this knowledge of our financial freedom if we continue in faith, confessing our freedom through the blood of mercy, we will surely win because we have already overcome.

John 16:33 – These things I have spoken unto you, that in me ye might have peace. In the world ye shall have tribulation: but be of good cheer; I have overcome the world.

Jesus upon the cross of Calvary has overcome life tribulations and trials for us, and this includes our financial life. We need to know these facts to be able to cope with the hardships that life sometimes throws at us. Work with the attitude and mentality that you have overcome that poverty trying to tire you down. Confess that you will get out of that debt and you will live a debt free life. You need to stand up to the devil that wealth is yours and he can't take it, you need to stand up for your right in Christ because nobody is going to help you. You know to reign as a king In live through Jesus Christ. Your financial situation cannot reign over you because mercy reign.

Romans 8:37 – Nay, in all these things we are more than conquerors through him that loved us.

The above scripture states that we are more than conqueror in Christ Jesus who loves us and gave his life for us. He died in your place, he gave up riches for you, he releases the power to get wealth to you, and he made you a joint heir with him by virtue of the blood of mercy. It will be a disaster if you depart this earth without using up all your financial inheritance in Christ Jesus. Most times we do not know what Jesus did on the cross of us, we do not know what price was paid, we do not know what gift were released, we do not know what dominion was transfer to us, we do not know who we even are in Him. There are lots of things we do not know because we need revelation to be able to believe. We might not know all but we just need to believe. Some of us because of laziness we forfeit our inheritance in the blood of mercy, even though mercy reign over our financial lives we still end up in serious poverty.

Proverbs 24:33 - Yet a little sleep, a little slumber, a little folding of the hands to sleep:

In that place for you to have a little sleep and a little slumber is all the enemy needs to put you in poverty. God has given you a zone to operate within, you need to find your zone and operate within it. Your zone is your place of expertise or an area where you are easily motivated to bring forth. You need to wake up to the fact that you have one life to live and must getup to do what God expect of you.

You can't afford a little sleep or little slumber because it will surely cost you what you will not be able to overcome. You are like a famer that after planting goes home to sleep. His crop will definitely be corrupted or destroy by the weeds. Though we don't see the lapse in our action when we go to a little sleep, the devil sees it and will surely take advantage of it.

It is written that "it is God that gives us the power to get wealth", that means no matter how much we struggle or work hard in life, without the anointing of God on our work, we work in vain and still remain in poverty. ***Deuteronomy 8:18 - But thou shalt remember the LORD thy God: for it is he that giveth thee power to get wealth, that he may establish his covenant which he sware unto thy fathers, as it is this day.*** This means there is no real riches outside the one that Christ has already provided through his blood. The riches through the blood of Jesus is the original riches that will not grow wings and fly away because the riches of the blood of Jesus is durable riches.

CHAPTER FIVE

MERCY REIGN: OVER SICKNESSES, DISEASES AND INFIRMITIES

According to Pastor Benny Hinn, Sickness is captivity. Sickness is bondage. Sickness is oppression!". How true this is when compare in line with the word of God, that Jesus went about doing good and healing those that were oppressed of the devil, this shows that sicknesses and diseases are from the devil and not God; it is also an oppression of the devil.

Act 10:13 - How God anointed Jesus of Nazareth with the Holy Ghost and with power: who went about doing good, and healing all that were oppressed of the devil; for God was with him.

Oppression is something that can lead to captivity, bondage and even death. God is concern about our freedom in him,

Psalm 16:11- You will show me the path of life; In Your presence is fullness of joy; At Your right hand are pleasures forevermore.

God is only about the business of divine health and that is why He sent His only son, our lord Jesus Christ to earth harmed with the balm of Gilead to heal all those that were already oppressed of the devil and then release an anointing for divine health for as many that will come under its umbrella or accept him as their lord and savior. Remember the Syrophenician woman whose daughter was sick and came to Jesus to help heal her daughter? Jesus said to her "healing is the children's bread" and you can't take what belongs to the children and give it to dogs. Mathew 15:22-29. This interaction between Jesus Christ and the Syrophenician woman reveals to us that it wasn't God's intention for any of His children to be sick; and since the devil has already inflicted sicknesses and diseases on the children of God because they sin against Him, there has to be a remedy – the blood of Jesus became that remedy, by the strip on the body of Jesus dripping with His own blood we were all cleanse from every form of sickness and diseases; we were set free from the oppression of the devil. Again, the discussion between Jesus and the Syrophenician woman also reveal that healing is for as many that believe in Him, that is, it is meant for the children. The blood of mercy reign over every form of sickness, disease or infirmity be it physical or spiritual.

ILLUSTRATION OF MATHEW 15:22-29

1. The syrophenician woman was an unbeliever, that is, wasn't a Christian.
2. She have faith that Jesus has the power to heal her sick daughter.
3. She believe that Jesus will have mercy on her despite she is not called a child.
4. Jesus confirmed that healing is for God's children
5. She revealed to us that if we persist in the place of prayer, we will receive our healing, despite our standing with the lord for He is merciful.
6. Jesus refer to healing as a food – bread, that means we ought to receive healing every day of our life.

From the above illustration, we could see that the mercy of God reign and prevail over whatever position we are with God, if Jesus liken the woman to a dog that means the children of God as heaven is concern are healed of every form of sickness or diseases but we need to say God's promises or words to that sickness.

MERCY REIGN OVER TIME OF ILLNESS IN OUR BODY

Some people believe that because they have had a particular illness for a long time, it is impossible for them to be healed. We know that there some characters listed in the bible that was ill some years and God healed them.

THE WOMAN WITH THE ISSUE OF BLOOD - The mercy of God goes beyond the number of years any sickness has lasted in our body; the woman with issue of blood has had that illness for 12 years with any hope of being cured but a day came she met with the God of mercy whose mercy reign above every sickness that night have been caused by sin and was healed delivered completely without a trace of the illness.

THE MADMAN OF GADARA –

THE MAN BY THE POOL –

THE WOMAN BIND BY THE DEVIL FOR 38 YEARS –

THE BLIND MAN EYES OPEN -

METHODS OF HEALING

Jesus used different methods in healing different type of sicknesses. We see that sometimes he laid hands on the sick, other times he spoke to the sickness and command it out of the person.

- Healing Prayer of Surrender
- Prayer of Reconciliation
- Healing Prayer of Command
- Prayer for a Creative Miracle

- Prayer to the Divine Physician
- Generational Healing Prayer
- Prayer for Inner Healing
- Prayer of Confirmation
- Prayer for Peaceful Rest

WAYS WE NEED TO WATCH OUR HEALTH

Healing is the children's bread. This is the idea that we understand from Jesus encounter with the Syrophenician woman. We are His children; the Lord's Prayer tells us to ask for daily bread. Because bread is a symbol for nourishment, we understand that we must believe for nourishment/healing daily.

Healing is to be taken into the body on a daily basis. We do this when we choose the right foods, the right vitamins, supplements, and herbs. We no longer live in the Garden of Eden; however God still 'gives us all things that pertain to life and godliness.' It is a bit harder than picking food off the trees, but the effort now will provide long term benefits as we age.

Lifestyle changes such as exercise and rest are also important to the restoration/regeneration of the body. We live in a very busy culture. There is something not quite right about taking time off, or pulling away to rest. Yet we find that when we do rest, we feel rejuvenated.

It is a challenge to put first things first, and carve out time from all the busy-ness to care for ourselves.

CHAPTER SIX

MERCY REIGN: OVER DEATH

Like sin, death also kneels before divine mercy in the promise of the resurrection. when Jesus resurrected he took over the keys of death from the devil, that means we as coheir with Christ Jesus now have authority over the spirit of death because key means authority.

In Isaiah 38, Hezekiah was very ill and a prophecy came from the lord that Hezekiah should put his house in order that he was going to die from the illness, but Hezekiah prayed unto the lord with weeping telling God how he has been faithful unto the work of God and his usefulness to things of God and the lord had mercy unto him and elongated his life with additional 15 years. Hezekiah did not pray, Lord, spare me; but, Lord, remember me; whether I live or die, let me be thine. God always hears the prayers of the broken in heart, and will give health, length of days, and temporal or permanent deliverance, as much and as long as is truly good for them. One important observation about this story is that, the same prophet God sent to tell Hezekiah of his death, the same prophet God sent to announce his healing and deliverance. The prophet did not get to his house when God spoke and asked him to go back to Hezekiah with His reply.

Isaiah 38:1-7 - In those days Hezekiah was sick and near death. And Isaiah the prophet, the son of Amoz, went to him and said to him, "Thus says the Lord: 'Set your house in order, for you shall die and not live.'"

2 Then Hezekiah turned his face toward the wall, and prayed to the Lord, 3 and said, "Remember now, O Lord, I pray, how I have walked before You in truth and with a loyal heart, and have done what is good in Your sight." And Hezekiah wept bitterly. 4 And the word of the Lord came to Isaiah, saying, 5 "Go and tell Hezekiah, 'Thus says the Lord, the God of David your father: "I have heard your prayer, I have seen your tears; surely I will add to your days fifteen years. 6 I will deliver you and this city from the hand of the king of Assyria, and I will defend this city."' 7 And this is the sign to you from the Lord, that the Lord will do this thing which He has spoken:

If God can change his own prophecy because he is a merciful God, how can He then not change an evil prophecy that is not from Him? God's answer to Hezekiah was so urgent that he asked Prophet Isaiah to go back to Hezekiah immediately.

Hezekiah upon hearing the merciful report of the lord, asked for a sign that truly he has been healed and he was given the sign. What a God we serve, a God that humility is His name; .God humble Himself by granting Hezekiah's request for a sign even after lifting the negative prophecy and healing him. He is a compassionate God and is able to pardon any sin or iniquity.

Our God is a merciful God and His mercy reigns above all negative prophecy; have there been any negative prophecy concerning you? Listen, the same God that had mercy on Hezekiah will have mercy on you.

In the new testament, we saw how Jesus Christ brought the dead back to life, Lazarus was dead for 4 days before Jesus got to him but at the end Jesus only gave thanks to God in heaven and called forth Lazarus from death back to life. What the death of Lazarus signifies is that it is not the will of God for man to die prematurely or untimely. The devil has design some people by his evil mark to die without fulfilling their purpose on earth by hastening their death. However,

God also design such occasion to glorify Himself. The mercy of God reign over death to frustrate the plans of the devil.

In the book of Luke 12:7 we were told of the widow who was on her way to the cemetery to bury her only son and child but Jesus passing by at the same hour stopped the bury procession and brought the boy back to life. I don't know what procession that is being held right now concerning you or any member of your family, Jesus is passing by and there will be a reverse of the event of that procession because the mercies of God reign above every untimely death. The blood of Jesus is able to speak to every physical and spiritual procession holding against you. Jesus went to the grave and taste death so that you and I will not taste death.

Luke 12:7 - Now when he came nigh to the gate of the city, behold, there was a dead man carried out, the only son of his mother, and she was a widow: and much people of the city was with her.

Apart from death of human, God's mercy can revive anything dead in your life. Whatever is looking like a bury procession right now in your life will receive heavenly attention very soon, Jesus is about to pass your way to that dead business, career, marriage, child misbehavior, relationship or whatever it is that you think cannot be revive.

In Matthew 9, Jairus comes to Jesus, falls to his knees and says that his daughter has died, Jairus was "a ruler of the synagogue," and a man of no small worldly means. Yet with all his possessions he was unable to do anything for his dear daughter's relief. His coming to Christ proves to us that he must have tried other means both high and low but all to no avail. The appearance and social position of Jesus did not stop him but rather he begged for his daughter to be brought back to life. Jaruis daughter was only 12 years old when she died; it makes one wonder why will children die? Have they sin also to warrant the penalty of death? John 10:10 says the devil comes but to steal, to kill and to destroy but Jesus came to give life abundantly. This is the main reason it is easy for Jesus to restore the dead back to life because he is the giver of life and the restore of whatever is lost or stolen. I want us to know that when Jaruis left his daughter to seek Jesus help, his daughter was still alive but a word was sent to him (while Jesus was being delayed on the way to his house by the woman with the issue of blood who touched Jesus garment and was made whole) that his daughter was dead. His faith was tried and while the sad news added the last pang to his sorrow, his faith did not weaken. Had not he sought the aid of One who had raised the widow's son at Nain? The mercy of God surpasses the pain we go through because we know and trust that he is able to ease our pain and we take solace in the fact that he will restore. I believe this was the case of Mr. Jaruis when he got the bad news that his sick daughter was actually dead. Jesus told him "Fear not, only believe", what a pillar to lean in times of trouble, what an encouraging words in the dark hour. THE MERCY OF God reigns in all situations and circumstance to bring healing, deliverance and peace to the weary souls.

Standing by the little bed, Jesus took one of the girl's cold hands in His and lovely said in her own Aramaic tongue, "Rise up, little maid!" the spirit of the dead girl quickened and she revived, saw the Saviour and got out of bed and walked. Luke the physician says, "Her spirit came again ... her parents and everyone present were surprised." Jesus gave a command that the grateful parents should not publicize the miracle in order to guard them against the temptation to talk unnecessarily about the wonderful event, and thereby lose the full benefit of the blessing they had received. WHAT POWER OF MERCY. I know that the power that raise Jesus from the grave with raise everything dead in your live. Where you have lost hope like Mr. Jaruis, I say to you like Jesus said to him, "fear not, and only believe".

PETER MOTHER IN LAW BROUGHT TO LIVE BY JESUS

SON OF THE SHUNEMITE WOMAN

LYDIA THE PURPLE SELLER

CHAPTER SEVEN

MERCY RELEASES UNSPEAKABLE JOY

The fall of man at the beginning resulted to man living a life of misery after they were driven out of the Garden of Eden before the fall, man had no misery since they lived in harmony with the lord but after the fall of man came misery and there was a reason for them to be restored. Misery is more than unhappiness, sorrow, or suffering. Misery is the ultimate state of disharmony with God and his laws. Jesus blood shed on the cross of Calvary brought about a new restoration to man's joy. The feeling of misery, depression or heaviness was taken away by the blood and man receives a new and energetic strength through the mercy of the blood which reigns over their misery; with joy we now return back to God.

Isaiah 61:3 - To appoint unto them that mourn in Zion, to give unto them beauty for ashes, the oil of joy for mourning, the garment of praise for the spirit of heaviness; that they might be called trees of righteousness, the planting of the LORD, that he might be glorified

Because of the mercy of theblood of jesus, there is grace for a new praise instead of the spirit of heaviness.

The book of Nehemiah 8:10 states that the joy of the lord is our strength, *10 Then he said unto them, Go your way, eat the fat, and drink the sweet, and send portions unto them for whom nothing is prepared: for this day is holy unto our Lord: neither be ye sorry; for the joy of the Lord is your strength.* Without the Joy of God we will not be able to function in any area of life. If the joy of God is our strength, then what happens when we lack God's joy? That means will not be able to function or dwell in the presence of the almighty God; neither shall we have the strength to carry on with our every-day life; because strength signifies our inner inspiration which spurs us to action in the outside. The Holy Spirit works in us through the lifeway of God's joy inside of us, this is the main reason Paul said we should not grieve the Holy Spirit; if we do, it will negatively affect every facet of our lives. Our prayers will be hinder and we will not be able to perform to our maximum or best.

In the book of Isaiah we were told that Jesus gave a new image/garment of joy and took away our old image of depression or heaviness. Part of the exchange that was done on the cross of Calvary is the exchange of depression and joy.

(Insert Bible verse)

The mercy of the blood of Jesus reign over every form of depression thereby releasing upon us His joy by virtue of the blood of mercy. This fact explain to us that our joy is not based on worldly stuff or affairs of this world but our joy comes flowing through the grace and mercy of the blood which reigns over our past, present and future circumstances or situation.

The mercy of the blood of Jesus releases unto us the divine joy from our lord Jesus which is first converted into a spiritual joy that is not visible and then converted again into a physical joy which reflect the strength we experience on the outside that is visible to the world – Blessing E. Bassey.

You can turn painful situation around through laughter. If you can find humor in anything, even poverty you can survive it – Bill Cosby.

Based on the scripture above (Nehemiah 8:10), we see how Nehemiah encourage the people to go their way, eat the best food they have prepare, drink the sweetest wine and above all send some portion to those that do not have because the joy of the lord is their strength. Joy not based on how much they have, or on how much their enemies terrorize them but a joy based on the assurance of the blood of Jesus for abundance, protection, security, peace, and so much more. When you have the joy of God no matter how little you have, you will still be looking for somebody who doesn't have for you to share with him/her. The joy of the lord makes you to see only abundance because in actual fact you are blessed. When you have the joy of the lord, the little you have becomes abundance and as you appreciate that little, with time it will grow from abundance to more abundance.

We are told by prophet Isaiah, that it is with joy we can draw water from the well of salvation, and we know that the well of salvation is where we find all kinds of blessings. The essence of this scripture is that where there is no joy of God, all other things or blessings will be hinder; the joy of God leads to the manifestation of other blessings. May God help us to experience His joy in our lives in Jesus name.

Isaiah 12:3 - Therefore with joy shall ye draw water out of the wells of salvation.

Nehemiah - 10 Then he said unto them, Go your way, eat the fat, and drink the sweet, and send portions unto them for whom nothing is prepared: for this day is holy unto our Lord: neither be ye sorry; for the joy of the Lord is your strength.

www.ingramcontent.com/pod-product-compliance
Lightning Source LLC
Chambersburg PA
CBHW070956120626

46546CB00004B/1649